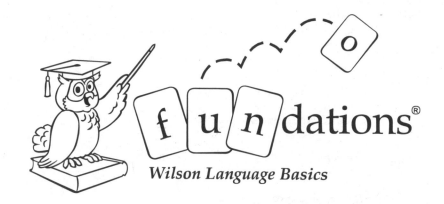

### Wilson Language Basics

# Student Notebook

## Level 3

**WILSON**®

*Wilson works*.

**SECOND EDITION**

Wilson Language Training Corporation

www.wilsonlanguage.com

www.fundations.com

**Fundations® Student Notebook 3**

Item # F2STNBK3

ISBN  978-1-56778-519-7

SECOND EDITION

PUBLISHED BY:

**Wilson Language Training Corporation**
47 Old Webster Road
Oxford, MA 01540
United States of America

(800) 899-8454

www.wilsonlanguage.com

Printed in the U.S.A.

August 2016

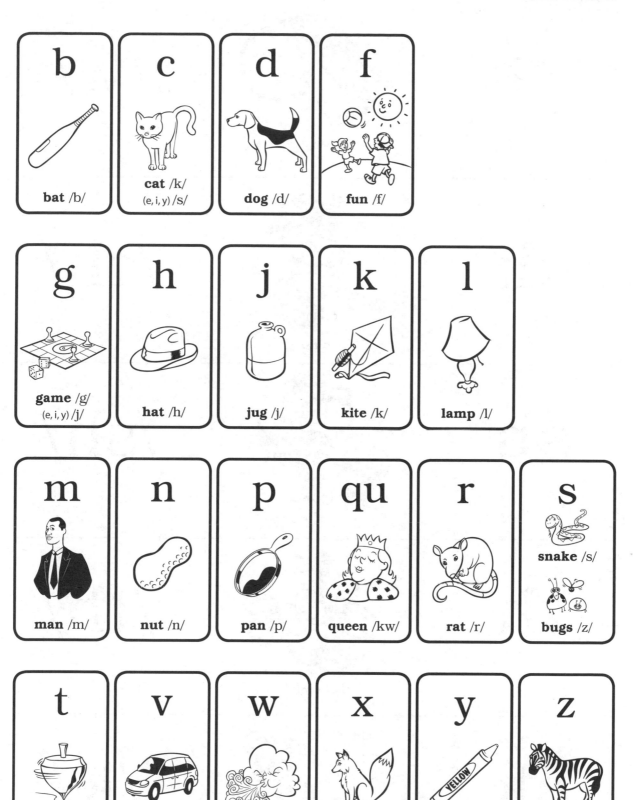

b — **bat** /b/

c — **cat** /k/ (e, i, y) /s/

d — **dog** /d/

f — **fun** /f/

g — **game** /g/ (e, i, y) /j/

h — **hat** /h/

j — **jug** /j/

k — **kite** /k/

l — **lamp** /l/

m — **man** /m/

n — **nut** /n/

p — **pan** /p/

qu — **queen** /kw/

r — **rat** /r/

s — **snake** /s/ **bugs** /z/

t — **top** /t/

v — **van** /v/

w — **wind** /w/

x — **fox** /ks/

y — **yellow** /y/

z — **zebra** /z/

**Digraphs**

| | | |
|---|---|---|
| wh | <br>whistle | /w/ |
| ch | <br>chin | /ch/ |
| sh | <br>ship | /sh/ |
| th | <br>thumb | /th/ |
| ck | 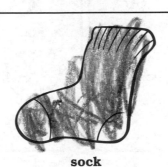<br>sock | /k/ |

| | | |
|---|---|---|
| tch | catch | /ch/ |
| dge | fudge | /j/ |
| tion | vacation | /shŭn/ |
| sion | mansion | /shŭn/ |
| sion | television | /zhŭn/ |
| ture | capture | /chər/ |
| tu | spatula | /chü/ |
| ci | glacier | /sh/ |
| ti | patient | /sh/ |

**Silent Letters**

| | | |
|---|---|---|
| wr | 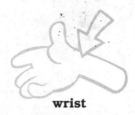<br>**wrist** | /r/ |
| rh | <br>**rhyme** | /r/ |
| gn | <br>**gnat** | /n/ |
| kn | 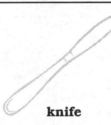<br>**knife** | /n/ |
| mn | <br>**column** | /m/ |
| mb | <br>**lamb** | /m/ |
| gh | <br>**ghost** | /g/ |

all /öl/

ball

an /an/

fan

am /am/

ham

| ng | nk |
|----|----|

ang /ang/

fang

ank /ank/

bank

ing /ing/

ring

ink /ink/

pink

ong /ong/

song

onk /onk/

honk

ung /ung/

lung

unk /unk/

junk

## Vowels in Closed Syllables

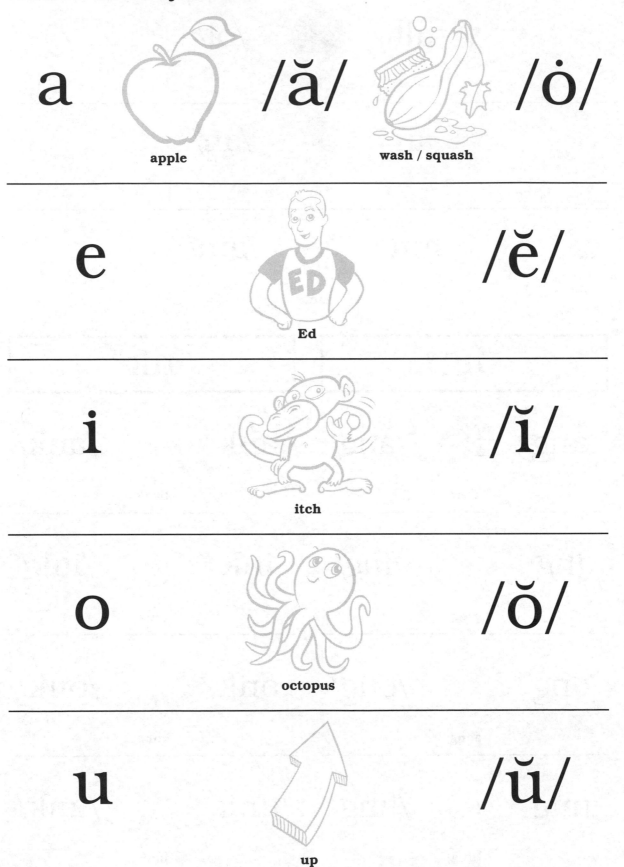

a    apple    /ă/    wash / squash    /ȯ/

e    Ed    /ĕ/

i    itch    /ĭ/

o    octopus    /ŏ/

u    up    /ŭ/

a  /ā/

safe

e  /ē/

Pete

i  /ī/

pine

o  /ō/

home

u  /ū/  /ü/

mule      rule

## Vowels In Open Syllables

a /ā/ /ŭ/

acorn      Alaska

e /ē/

me

i /ī/ /ŭ/or /ĭ/ /ē/

hi      animal      champion

o /ō/

no

u /ū/ /ü/

pupil      flu

y  /ī/ /ē/

cry      baby

# Vowels

| Vowel | Closed Syllable | Vowel-Consonant-e Syllable | Vowel-Open Syllable |
|-------|-----------------|----------------------------|---------------------|
| a | apple /ă/   **wash** squash /ŏ/ | safe /ā/ | acorn /ā/   Alaska /ŭ/ |
| e | Ed /ĕ/ | Pete /ē/ | me /ē/ |
| i | itch /ĭ/ | pine /ī/ | hi /ī/   **animal** /ŭ/ or /ĭ/   champion /ē/ |
| o | octopus /ŏ/ | home /ō/ | no /ō/ |
| u | up /ŭ/ | mule /ū/   rule /ü/ | pupil /ū/   flu /ü/ |
| y | | | cry /ī/   baby /ē/ |

**Closed Syllable Exceptions**

ind  /īnd/

find

ild  /īld/

wild

old  /ōld/

cold

olt  /ōlt/

colt

ost  /ōst/

post

**Vowel-Consonant-e Exception**

ive  /ĭv/

give

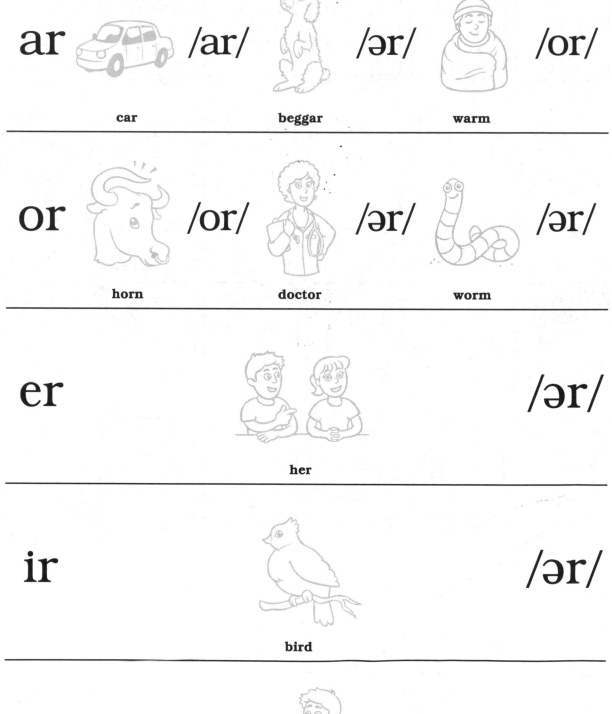

ar /ar/ /ər/ /or/

car    beggar    warm

or /or/ /ər/ /ər/

horn    doctor    worm

er /ər/

her

ir /ər/

bird

ur /ər/

burn

## Vowel Teams

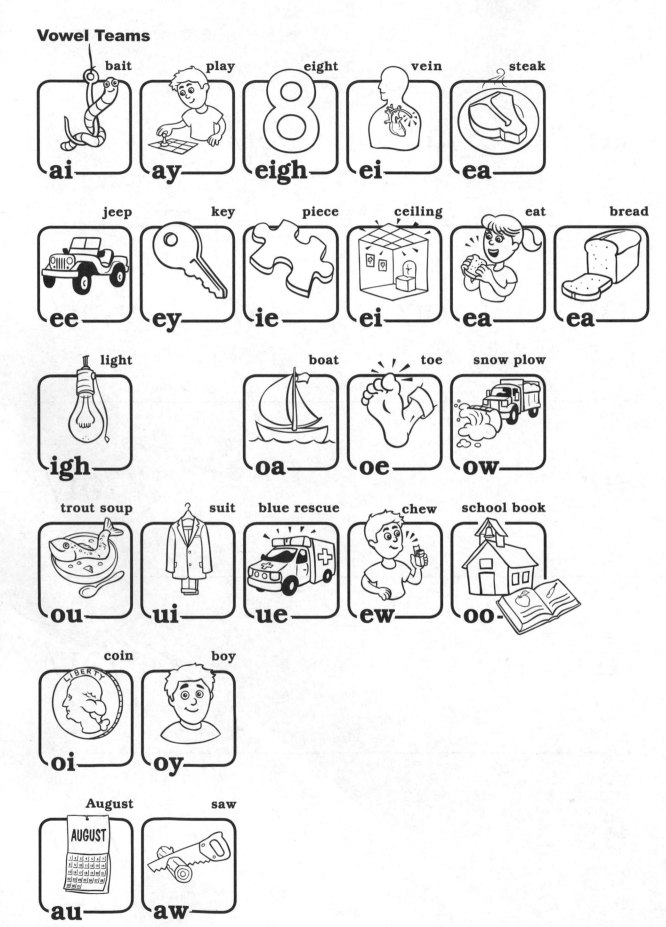

bait — **ai**
play — **ay**
eight — **eigh**
vein — **ei**
steak — **ea**

jeep — **ee**
key — **ey**
piece — **ie**
ceiling — **ei**
eat — **ea**
bread — **ea**

light — **igh**
boat — **oa**
toe — **oe**
snow plow — **ow**

trout soup — **ou**
suit — **ui**
blue rescue — **ue**
chew — **ew**
school book — **oo**

coin — **oi**
boy — **oy**

August — **au**
saw — **aw**

## Vowel Teams

| | | |
|---|---|---|
| ai | \n\nbait | /ā/ |
| ay | \n\nplay | /ā/ |
| ee | \n\njeep | /ē/ |
| ea | \n\neat | /ē/ |
| ey | \n\nkey | /ē/ |

**Vowel Teams**

oi  /oi/

coin

oy  /oi/

boy

oa  /ō/

boat

oe  /ō/

toe

ow  /ō/ /ou/

snow    plow

ou  /ou/ /ü/

trout      soup

oo  /ü/ /ü/

school      book

ue  /ü/ /ū/

blue      rescue

ew  /ü/

chew

**Vowel Teams**

au  /ȯ/

August

aw  /ȯ/

saw

eigh 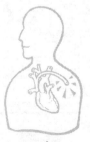 /ā/

eight

ei  /ā/

vein

ea  /ā/  /ĕ/

steak      bread

**Vowel Teams**

ie  /ē/

piece

ei  /ē/

ceiling

igh  /ī/

light

ui  /ü/

suit

**Spelling Options**

| /w/ | → | ☐ wind | ☐ whistle |
| /z/ | → | ☐ zebra | ☐ bugs, wise |
| /t/ | → | ☐ top | ☐ jumped |
| /s/ | → | ☐ snake | ☐ followed by e, i, y |
| /d/ | → | ☐ dog | ☐ thrilled |
| /j/ | → | ☐ jug | ☐ followed by e, i, y |
| | | ☐ fudge | |
| /f/ | → | ☐ fan | ☐ phone |
| /k/ | → | ☐ cat | ☐ kite |
| | | ☐ sock | ☐ chorus |
| /ch/ | → | ☐ chin | ☐ catch |
| | | ☐ spatula /chü/ | ☐ capture /chər/ |

**Spelling Options**

/shŭn/ → ☐ vacation ☐ mansion

/g/ → ☐ game ☐ ghost

/r/ → ☐ rat ☐ wrist

☐ rhyme

/n/ → ☐ nut ☐ gnat

☐ knife

/m/ → ☐ man ☐ column

☐ lamb

/sh/ → ☐ ship ☐ patient

☐ glacier

**Spelling Options for Vowel Sounds**

| /ər/ | er | ir | ur | ar | or |
|---|---|---|---|---|---|

| /ā/ | a-e | a | ai | ay | eigh | ei | ea |
|---|---|---|---|---|---|---|---|

| /ē/ | e-e | e | y | i | ee | ey | ea | ie | ei |
|---|---|---|---|---|---|---|---|---|---|

| /ī/ | i-e | i | y | igh |
|---|---|---|---|---|

| /ō/ | o-e | o | oa | oe | ow |
|---|---|---|---|---|---|

| /ū/ | u-e | u | ue |
|---|---|---|---|

| /ü/ | u-e | u | ue | ew | ou | oo | ui |
|---|---|---|---|---|---|---|---|

| /oi/ | oi | oy |
|---|---|---|

| /ou/ | ow | ou |
|---|---|---|

| /ȯ/ | a | au | aw |
|---|---|---|---|

Wilson Fundations® | ©2005, 2012 Wilson Language Training Corporation

**SYLLABLES**

## What is a Syllable?

A syllable is a word or part of a word made by **one push of breath**.

A syllable must have a least **one vowel**.

| | |
|---|---|
| **closed syllable** | 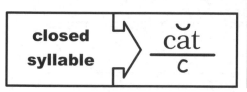 |

**Exception**

| | |
|---|---|
| **v-e syllable** |  |

**Exception**

| | |
|---|---|
| **open syllable** |  |

**Exception** **Exception** **Exception**

| | |
|---|---|
| **-le syllable** | 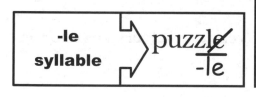 |

**Exception**

| | |
|---|---|
| **r-controlled syllable** | 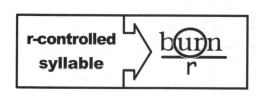 |

**Exception**
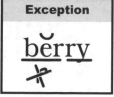

| | |
|---|---|
| **"D" syllable** | 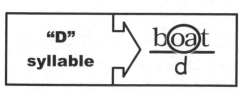 |

**Exception**

## Closed Syllables

**1.** This syllable can only have **one vowel**.

**2.** The vowel is followed by **one** or **more consonants** (closed in).

**3.** The vowel sound is **short**. To indicate the short sound, the vowel is marked with a breve ( ˘ ).

**4.** This syllable can be combined with other syllables to make **multisyllabic** words.

**Exceptions: ind, ild, old, olt, ost** words

The vowel is usually long even though it is in a closed syllable.

In words with unaccented closed syllables, the unaccented vowel might be a **schwa**. **Schwa** at the end of a word, spell with **e** or **o**.

**Schwa** at the end of a word saying **/ət/**, spell with **et**.

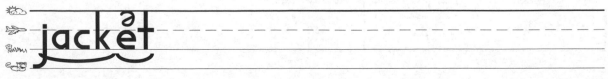

# Vowel-Consonant-e Syllables

1. This syllable has a **vowel**, then a **consonant**, then an **e**.

2. The first vowel is **long**. To indicate the long sound, the vowel is marked with a macron ( ˉ ).

3. The **e** is silent.

4. This syllable can be combined with other syllables to make **multisyllabic** words.

**Exceptions:** the letter **v**

Sometimes a word has a **vowel**, a **v**, then an **e**. The **e** may make the vowel long (**five**), or it may be there because English words do not end in a **v**. The vowel sound may still be short.

## Open Syllables

1. This syllable has only **one vowel** which is the last letter in the syllable.

2. The vowel sound is **long**. To indicate the long sound, the vowel is marked with a macron ( - ).

3. This syllable can be combined with other syllables to make **multisyllabic** words.

**Exceptions:** The vowel in an unstressed or unaccented open syllable has a **schwa**. This happens with **a** at the beginning or end of a word.

It happens with **i** in the middle syllable, when the **i** is followed by a **consonant**.

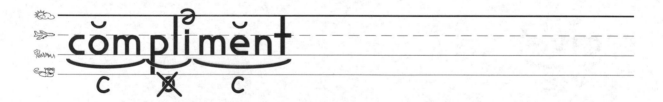

When the **i** is followed by a **vowel**, it often says /ĕ/.

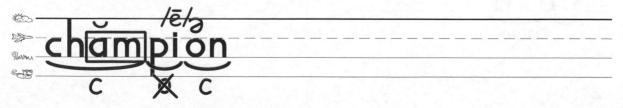

# Final Stable Syllable

## Consonant -le Syllable

**1.** This syllable has only three letters: a **consonant**, an **l**, and an **e**.

**2.** The **e** is silent. It is the vowel. Every syllable needs at least one vowel. The consonant and the l are sounded like a blend.

**3.** This syllable must be the last syllable in a **multisyllabic** word.

**Exceptions:** When a word ends in **stle**, *both* the **t** and the **e** are silent.

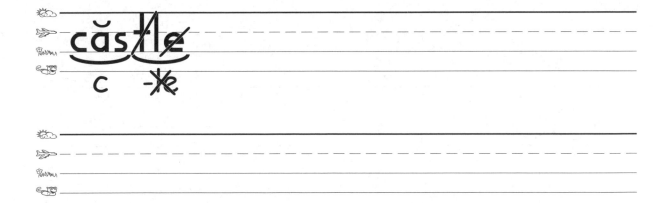

# R-Controlled Syllables

1. This syllable contains a single vowel followed by an **r** (**ar, er, ir, or, ur**).

2. The vowel is neither **long** nor **short**; it is controlled by the **r**.

3. This syllable can be combined with other syllables to make **multisyllabic** words.

**Exceptions: rr**

When a vowel is followed by a double **r** (**rr**), the vowel before it might have a short sound.

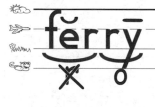

# Vowel Digraph / Diphthong ("D" Syllables)

**1.** This syllable contains a **vowel digraph** or a **diphthong**. These are vowel teams.

**Vowel Digraph:**
Two vowels together that represent one sound (**ee**)

**Diphthong:**
A sound that begins with one vowel sound and glides into another (**oi**)

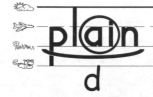

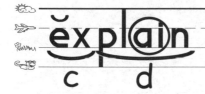

**Exceptions:** Sometimes two vowels together do not form a vowel team. The two vowels are split and the word is divided into syllables between the two vowels.

## Spelling Rules

### Four Ways to Spell /k/ = c, k, ck, ch

c    **cat**    /k/

Use **c** at the beginning of most words.

c̲at

Use **c** when the /k/ sound is the first letter of a blend.

c̲rash/ac̲t

Use **c** in multisyllabic words ending with **ic**.

picnic̲

---

k    **kite**    /k/

Use **k** in glued sounds with **nk**.

st̲ink

Use **k** when the /k/ sound is the last letter of the blend.

mil̲k̲

Use **k** in vowel-consonant-e words.

bik̲e

---

ck    **sock**    /k/

Use **ck** at the end of a one syllable word, right after the vowel.

soc̲k̲

pic̲k̲

Use **ck** in compound words.

humpbac̲k̲

---

ch    **chorus**    /k/

Use **ch** at the beginning of some words and with some /**sk**/ blends.

c̲horus

sc̲hool

---

SPELLING

28    Wilson Fundations® | ©2005, 2012 Wilson Language Training Corporation

# Spelling with ck and tch

 ## Spelling with ck

At the end of a one syllable word, use **ck** right after a short vowel. After a consonant, use **k**.

| Words with k | Words with ck |
|---|---|
| silk | block |
| mask | tackle |

 ## Spelling with tch

At the end of a one syllable word, use **tch** right after a short vowel. After a consonant, use **ch**.

| Words with ch | Words with tch |
|---|---|
| inch | match |
| munch | itch |

es

ing

ed /əd/ /t/ /d/

er

est

ish

able

en

ive

y

or

s /s/ /z/

ful

less

ness

ment

ly

ty

ward

# The Baseword/Suffix Rules -s and -es

 ## Baseword

A **baseword** is a word that can stand alone as a word or have something added to it.

## Suffix

A **suffix** is an ending that can be added to a baseword.

 ## Plurals

A **plural** word is a word that means more than one thing. Nouns add **s** or **es** to make them plural.

 ## Action Words

The **s** or **es** are also added to an **action** baseword or other verbs.

| Plurals | Action Words |
|---------|--------------|
| <u>bug</u>ⓢ | <u>sip</u>ⓢ |

Nouns and verbs ending in **s**, **x**, **z**, **ch**, **tch** and **sh** add **es**.

| | |
|---------|--------------|
| <u>lunch</u>ⓔⓢ | <u>mix</u>ⓔⓢ |

# Irregular Plurals

Some nouns have unusual or irregular plurals. The words below are some of the most common ones.

 ### Words ending in f or fe, change f to v and add es or s:

half, wolf ➜ halves, wolves

wife, life, knife ➜ wives, lives, knives

loaf ➜ loaves

 ### Words ending in o, add es:

potato, tomato, volcano ➜ potatoes, tomatoes, volcanoes

 ### Words that change from the original word:

| man ➜ men | woman ➜ women | child ➜ children |
| tooth ➜ teeth | foot ➜ feet | mouse ➜ mice |

 ### Words that do not change:

| fish ➜ fish | deer ➜ deer | sheep ➜ sheep |

SPELLING

# Understanding Suffixes

| Meaning | Suffix/Example | Part of Speech |
|---|---|---|
| **Indicates when something is or has been done** | **ing: disrupting**<br>is doing this now | verb |
| | **ed: disrupted**<br>already did in past | verb |
| **Comparing things** | **er: quicker**<br>describes something that is more quick than one other thing | adjective |
| | **est: quickest**<br>describes something that is "the most" quick (3 or more things) | adjective |
| **With or without** | **less: thankless**<br>without any thanks | adjective |
| | **ful: thankful**<br>with much thanks | adjective |
| **Person doing something** | **er: golfer**<br>person who golfs | noun |
| | **or: inspector**<br>person who inspects | noun |
| **Having the nature or quality of, or "being like" the basewords** | **ish: childish**<br>being like a child | adjective |
| | **ive: disruptive**<br>having nature to disrupt | adjective |
| | **y: risky**<br>describes something that has risk | adjective |
| | **ly: quickly**<br>doing something with a quick nature | adverb |
| | **ty: loyalty**<br>the state or quality of being loyal | noun |
| | **ness: kindness**<br>the quality of being kind | noun |
| **Other** | **able: washable**<br>capable of being washed | adjective |
| | **en: sharpen**<br>to make or become sharp | verb |
| | **ment: statement**<br>the act of stating | noun |

# Advanced Vowel Suffixes

The following vowel suffixes can be word endings. These suffix endings actually become part of the last syllable!

| | words with ti | words with ci |
|---|---|---|
| **al /əl/** | | |
| **ent /ĕnt/** | | |
| **ous /ŭs/** | | |
| **an /ăn/** | | |
| **er /ər/** | | |

# The 1-1-1 Doubling Rule

 ### Doubling Words

1-1-1 words are closed or r-controlled words with 1 syllable, 1 vowel, and 1 consonant after the vowel.

**Example:**   ship + ing = shipping

When adding a vowel suffix to a 1-1-1 doubling baseword, double the final consonant.

cup + ed =

flat + est =

star + ing =

When adding a consonant suffix to a 1-1-1 doubling baseword, just add the suffix.

cup + ful =

flat + ly =

ship + ment =

The consonants **h**, **j**, **k**, **v**, **w**, **x** and **y** do not double in English words.

# The Silent e and Suffix Rule

 **Adding a Suffix**

When adding a vowel suffix to a baseword ending in **e**, drop the **e**.

glide + ing =

dance + er =

live + ing =

juggle + ing =

When adding a consonant suffix to a baseword ending in **e**, just add the suffix.

like + ly =

life + less =

This rule also applies to words ending in a consonant -le syllable.

settle + ing =

settle + ment =

**SPELLING**

# The y and Suffix Rule

 ## Following a Consonant

If **y** follows a consonant in an open syllable, change **y** to **i** when adding *any* suffix. The **i** retains the original sound of the **y**.

cry + ed =

empty + ed =

tidy + ness =

empty + ness =

## Suffix Plus Suffix

If the **y** suffix is added to a baseword and then another suffix is added, change the **y** suffix to **i** and add the other suffix.

**Example:** dirt + y = dirty      dirty + est = dirtiest

dirty + est =

lonely + ness =

**Exception:** When the suffix begins with **i**, do not change the **y** to **i**, just add the suffix.

baby + ish =

# The y and Suffix Rule (continued)

 ## Forming Plurals

When forming plurals, change **y** to **i** and add **es**. The **-es** suffix says **/z/**.

**Example:** baby = babies

penny = _____

lady = _____

 ## D Syllable

If **y** is part of a dipthong or vowel digraph ("D" Syllable), just add the suffix.

play + ed = _____

volley + ing = _____

play + ful = _____

employ + ment = _____

SPELLING

## Making Contractions

**1.** Identify the two words you are putting together.

**2.** Take letters away from the 2nd word - **never the first!** Put the apostrophe in the place of the missing letters.

| When Contracting: | Take Away: | is not = |
|---|---|---|
| not | o | |

|  | not no**'t** |  | not no**'t** |  | have ha**'ve** |
|---|---|---|---|---|---|
| **are** | are not aren't | **had** | had not hadn't | **could** | could have could've |
| **can** | can not can't | **has** | has not hasn't | **should** | should have should've |
| **could** | could not couldn't | **have** | have not haven't | **would** | would have would've |
| **did** | did not didn't | **is** | is not isn't | | |
| **does** | does not doesn't | **was** | was not wasn't | | |
| **should** | should not shouldn't | **were** | were not weren't | | |
| **might** | might not mightn't | **would** | would not wouldn't | | |
| **must** | must not mustn't | | | | |

**Special cases:**   will not = won't         let us = let's
do not = don't         I am = I'm

# Making Contractions (continued)

|  | is<br>i**'s** | are<br>a**'re** | will<br>wi**'ll** | would<br>woul**'d** | have/has<br>ha**'ve**/ha**'s** | had<br>ha**'d** |
|---|---|---|---|---|---|---|
| **I** | – | – | I will<br>I'll | I would<br>I'd | I have<br>I've | I had<br>I'd |
| **it** | it is<br>it's | – | it will<br>it'll | – | it has<br>it's | – |
| **he** | he is<br>he's | – | he will<br>he'll | he would<br>he'd | he has<br>he's | he had<br>he'd |
| **she** | she is<br>she's | – | she will<br>she'll | she would<br>she'd | she has<br>she's | she had<br>she'd |
| **that** | that is<br>that's | – | – | – | that has<br>that's | – |
| **they** | – | they are<br>they're | they will<br>they'll | they would<br>they'd | they have<br>they've | they had<br>they'd |
| **we** | – | we are<br>we're | we will<br>we'll | we would<br>we'd | we have<br>we've | we had<br>we'd |
| **what** | what is<br>what's | what are<br>what're | what will<br>what'll | – | what has<br>what's | – |
| **where** | where is<br>where's | – | – | – | – | – |
| **who** | who is<br>who's | – | who will<br>who'll | who would<br>who'd | who has<br>who's | who had<br>who'd |
| **you** | – | you are<br>you're | you will<br>you'll | you would<br>you'd | you have<br>you've | you had<br>you'd |

## Common Prefixes

 **Prefix**

A **prefix** is a word part that is placed before a baseword or a root to provide meaning.

**Example:**  unkind      un = prefix added to kind

### Common Prefixes

**Closed Syllable**

| Prefix | Meaning |
|--------|---------|
| con | with or together |
| *dis, un | not, opposite of |
| en, em | in, into, cause to |
| ex | out of, away from |
| *in-im-il-ir | not |
| mis | wrongly, bad |
| non | not |
| sub | under |
| trans | across, beyond |

**Open Syllable**

| Prefix | Meaning |
|--------|---------|
| de | opposite |
| e | out of, away |
| pre | before |
| pro | in favor of/ move forward |
| *re | again |

*These prefixes make up 97% of prefixed words in English!

Example of closed syllable prefix:

Example of open syllable prefix:

SPELLING

# Common Roots

 **Root**

A **root** is the basic element of a word, and it is the foundation on which the meaning of a word is built.

## Common Roots

| Root | Meaning |
|------|---------|
| dict | speak |
| duct | lead, guide |
| fect | make |
| fract | break |
| ject | throw |
| junct | join |
| lect | choose |

| Root | Meaning |
|------|---------|
| min | little, small |
| scrib | write |
| sist | to make firm, to stay |
| spec | see, look |
| struct | build |
| tract | drag |

Examples of prefix + root word:

## Spelling Options

SPELLING OPTIONS

# A

able
absent
accident
ache
actor
actual
adoption
advanced
adventure
advice
age
agriculture
ahead
alphabet
already
ambulance
anchor
anchored
ankle
ankles
ape
apologize
apology
apple
apples
armor
artificial
atmosphere
atrocious
aunt
autumn

# B

bagel
bake
balance
bandit
banker
base
baseword
basket
battle
beaver
belief
believe
below
beneath
bike
birch
bird
birth
bite
blaze
blister
blue
bone
boost
Boston
bottle
brace
braced
brain
bread
break
breakfast

# B

breath
bright
bronchitis
brown
brownie
Bruce
bucket
bugle
bugles
bundle
burn
burp

# C

cable
cage
cake
calendar
came
camel
cancel
candle
candles
cane
capture
care
cartoon
cashier
castle
cautious
cave
cent
channel
chaos
chapel
chapter
character
cheap
chemical
chief
chimney
chirp
choke
chorus
chose
Chris

# C

chrome
church
cinch
Cindy
cite
citizen
city
close
coat
collar
column
communication
competition
complain
comprise
concentrate
concentration
concept
conception
condition
conductor
cone
confer
confuse
congratulate
constitution
construction
convinced
convincing
cookie
corner
cradle

# C

cradles
crayon
craze
creature
cricket
crow
crucial
crumb
crumble
crumbling
cube
cuddle
cuddled
cuddles
culture
curl
cursive
curtsy
cycle

**Spelling Options**

# D

dancer
dancing
dangle
dare
death
decide
decision
definition
delicious
delight
delighted
delightful
denim
departure
description
detection
dial
dictation
diet
dime
dimple
dirt
dirty
distribution
disturb
dive
doctor
doe
dollar
dolphin
donkey
doze

# D

dragon
drawn
drew
dribble
drive
drizzle
drizzled
drizzles
drizzling
dumb

# E

echo
education
eight
eighty
electrician
elevator
embrace
emerge
emotion
enforce
entertain
entrance
erosion
estimation
eventually
example
exceed
expansion
expert
export
expose
extension

# F

face
facial
facing
factor
factual
falcon
fancy
favor
feather
feature
fee
fences
fender
fern
fiction
fiddle
field
fierce
fight
file
final
financial
fir
fire
first
fizzle
flame
flavor
flea
flew
flight
flow

# F

flute
foam
formula
fortune
fracture
freckle
freckles
freight
freighter
fright
frighten
frontier
frown
froze
fruit
fumble
fumbled
fumbling
function
furniture
fuse

# G

gable
gem
genie
gentle
gentleman
ghost
ghostly
ghoul
giant
gigantic
giggle
giggled
giggles
giggling
girl
glacial
globe
glow
glue
goalie
gobble
governor
Grace
graceful
gracefully
gracious
grade
grape
graze
great
greatly
groan

**GHIJKL**

# G

grow
grumble
guzzle

# H

habit
handle
handling
harbor
haul
haze
head
headlight
headmaster
healthy
heavy
helmet
helmets
her
hide
high
highway
hobble
hole
home
hope
huddle
huddles
huge
hugely
hurt
hustle

# I

ice
identification
impatient
indeed
infection
infectious
infer
initial
initiate
innovation
insert
inside
inspection
inspector
instead
instruction
instructor
interact
invention
inventor
investigation
isolation

# J

jacket
jackets
janitor
jingle
joke
Joseph
juggle
juggler
juggles
jumble
jumper
jungle

# K

kite
knapsack
knee
kneecap
kneel
knew
knickers
knickknack
knife
knight
knighthood
knit
knitting
knives
knob
knock
knot
known

# L

label
lace
lake
lamb
lane
lantern
leather
legal
lemon
level
lice
license
light
lightning
like
limb
lime
limit
line
little
littlest
lobster
location
locket
lotion
louder

# M

magician
magnet
magnets
maintain
major
mansion
mantel
manufacture
maple
maples
martial
Martian
masterpiece
mathematician
mature
maze
meadow
meant
mechanical
melodies
melon
mental
mention
mermaid
middle
might
mighty
mildew
mile
mine
minimal
minor

# M

mixture
model
moisture
monitor
monster
moody
moonlight
motor
mow
mule
musician
muzzle

# N

name
Nancy
nation
nature
neigh
neighbor
neighborhood
network
nibble
nice
nicely
nicest
nickel
night
nightingale
nightmare
nine
noble
nose
note
notebook
notion
novel
numb
nutritious

# O

optician
option
orchestra
orchid
outfield
own
oxen

# P

pace
pacing
packet
paddle
page
pamphlet
panel
panther
partial
partner
pasture
patient
peasant
pebble
pebbles
pencil
percent
perfect
perfume
persist
phone
phonics
phony
photo
photograph
pickles
picture
piece
pile
place
placed
placement

# P

plane
planet
planets
plaster
plate
pleasant
plumber
pocket
pocketbook
poke
pole
politician
pollen
popular
portion
Portugal
pose
position
posture
potential
prairie
precious
presidential
pretzel
prevention
price
priced
priceless
principal
problem
proceed
production

**M N O P Qu R S**

MNOPQuRS

| P | Q | R |
|---|---|---|
| promotion | quake | rabbit |
| proportion | queen | racket |
| protection | question | raffle |
| prune | quicker | rainbow |
| publication | | Ralph |
| puddle | | rattle |
| puddles | | razor |
| punctuate | | read |
| puzzle | | ready |
| puzzles | | recent |
| | | recite |
| | | rectangle |
| | | regular |
| | | rejection |
| | | relaxation |
| | | relief |
| | | relieve |
| | | remodel |
| | | replace |
| | | replacement |
| | | replacing |
| | | rescue |
| | | return |
| | | reveal |
| | | revolution |
| | | rhinestone |
| | | rhinoceros |
| | | rhubarb |
| | | rice |
| | | ride |
| | | ripe |
| | | roast |

# R

rocket
rockets
rookie
rooster
rope
rose
ruby
ruffle
rule
ruler

# S

salad
sale
sample
sandal
schedule
scheme
school
schooner
scrabble
scramble
scrape
scribble
scribbles
scrumptious
sculpture
section
seek
selection
sentence
sequential
serve
settle
settlement
settles
settling
seven
share
sheet
shine
shirt
shopper
shriek

# S

shrivel
sigh
signal
signature
silly
similar
simple
simplest
since
sincere
singer
single
sir
sizzle
sizzlcr
skirt
sleigh
slice
sliced
slide
slope
smile
snake
sniffle
sniffles
snowed
snuggle
snuggles
social
softer
solar
solution

**MNOPQuRS**

TUVWXYZ

## S

soup
space
spacecraft
spaced
spacious
spatial
spatula
special
spice
spicy
spider
spine
spoke
spoon
spread
sprinkle
sprinkler
sprinkles
spruce
squabble
squirm
stable
stables
stage
staple
stapled
stapler
state
statue
steady
stencil

## S

stew
stingy
stir
stomach
street
structure
strudel
struggle
struggled
struggling
study
stumble
sturdy
subtraction
sufficient
suggest
suggestion
suit
summit
sunrise
surf
surprise
survive
suspension
suspicious
swear
sweat
sweater
sweating
swirl
swivel

## T

table
tables
tackle
talent
tangle
tape
tarantula
target
tattle
tattled
tattles
team
tear
technical
telephone
television
temper
temperature
temptation
tension
term
termite
Texas
these
thief
thimble
thirsty
thirteen
thirty
those
thread

# T

thriller
throne
thrown
thumb
thunder
ticket
tickle
tickles
tickling
tide
tight
tiptoe
title
toe
tonsil
tooth
tow
trace
tractor
trade
tradition
train
trample
travel
tremble
trickle
triumph
trophy
true
trumpet
tube

# T

tumble
tumbles
tune
turkey
turn
turnips
twice
twilight
twinkle
twirl

# U

understood
use

**TUVWXYZ**

**Spelling Options**

TUVWXYZ

# V

velvet
verb
vicious
vinegar
violation
virtual
vote
vulture

# W

waddle
waffle
wagon
Walter
wander
wave
wealthy
wear
weather
weigh
weight
weightless
whale
whine
whirl
whistle
white
wide
wife
wiggle
wiggled
wiggles
wince
wincing
window
wine
wipe
wise
word
work
workbench

# W

workbook
worker
world
worldly
worldwide
worm
wormy
worst
worth
worthwhile
worthy
wrap
wreath
wreck
wrecker
wren
wrench
wrestle
wriggle
wring
wrinkles
wrist
write
wrong

**Vocabulary**

# Aa

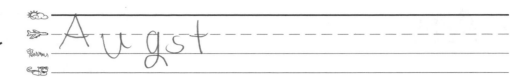

Augst

Augst is still summer!

# Aa

# Aa

VOCABULARY

**Vocabulary**

Aa

Aa

Bb

Wilson Fundations® | ©2005, 2012 Wilson Language Training Corporation

**Vocabulary**

# Bb

# Bb

# Bb

**Vocabulary**

Cc  crunch

I want a crunchy cooke

Cc

Cc

# Cc

# Cc

# Cc

**Vocabulary**

Cc

Cc

Cc

# Cc

# Cc

# Cc

**Vocabulary**

Dd

Dd

Dd

**Vocabulary**

# Dd

# Ee

# Ee

**Vocabulary**

# Ee

# Ff

# Gg

Wilson Fundations® | ©2005, 2012 Wilson Language Training Corporation

# Hh

# Hh

# Hh

**Vocabulary**

# Hh

# Hh

# Ii

**Ii**

**GHIJKL**

**Ii**

**Jj**

**Vocabulary**

# Kk

# Ll

# Ll

Wilson Fundations® | ©2005, 2012 Wilson Language Training Corporation

# Mm

MNOPQuRS

# Mm

# Mm

# Mm

# Nn

# Oo

# Pp

# Pp

# Pp

MNOPQuRS

# Pp

# Rr

# Rr

# Rr

# Ss

scold

Mom always scolds at

me.

# Ss

**S s**

**S s**

**S s**

# S s

# S s

# S s

MNOPQuRS

# Vocabulary

## S s

Wilson Fundations® | ©2005, 2012 Wilson Language Training Corporation

## Ss

## Ss

## Ss

**Vocabulary**

# T t

# T t

# V v

Wilson Fundations® | ©2005, 2012 Wilson Language Training Corporation

# Vv

# Ww

Watch

I don't waut to play

I want to watch tv

# Ww

TUVWXYZ

**Vocabulary**

# Ww

# Ww

# Ww

Wilson Fundations® | ©2005, 2012 Wilson Language Training Corporation

**Trick Words**

# A

a
about
again
against
also
always
America
and
animal
another
answer
any
are
as
August
away

# B

be
beautiful
been
being
between
both
bought
breakfast
brother
brought
by

# C

called
carry
change
city
come
could
country
couple
cousin

# D

daughter
day
December
different
do
does
done
down

# E

each
early
earth
eight
enough
every

# F

family
father
favorite
February
first
for
friend
from
full

_____
_____
_____
_____
_____
_____
_____

_____
_____
_____
_____
_____
_____
_____

_____
_____
_____
_____
_____
_____
_____

# G

goes
good
great

# H

has
have
he
head
her
here
his
house
how

# I

I
into
is

# J

January
July

_____

_____

_____

_____

_____

_____

# K

knew
know

_____

_____

_____

_____

_____

_____

# L

large
laugh
learn
little
look
lose

_____

_____

_____

_____

_____

_____

## Trick Words

MNOPQuRS

| M | N | O |
|---|---|---|
| many | new | ocean |
| may | night | of |
| me | none | often |
| Monday | nothing | once |
| month | now | one |
| mother | number | only |
| move | | or |
| Mr. | | other |
| Mrs. | | our |
| my | | out |
| | | over |
| | | own |

| P | R | S |
|---|---|---|
| people | ready | said |
| picture | right | Saturday |
| piece | | say |
| place | | says |
| please | | school |
| pretty | | see |
| pull | | shall |
| put | | she |
| | | should |
| | | something |
| | | some |
| | | son |
| | | special |
| | | sure |

_____ _____ _____

_____ _____ _____

_____ _____ _____

_____ _____ _____

_____ _____ _____

_____ _____ _____

_____ _____ _____

_____ _____ _____

**M N O P Qu R S**

## Trick Words

# T

talk
the
their
there
they
thought
Thursday
together
to
tomorrow
too
trouble
try
Tuesday
two

# U

use
used

# V

very

# W

walk
want
was
water
way
we
Wednesday
were
what
when
where
who
whose
why
won
word
work
world
would
write

# Y

you
young
your

_____

_____

_____

_____

_____

_____

_____

**Sound Alikes**

# A
## ate
eight

_____

_____

_____

_____

# B
## band
banned

_____

_____

_____

## banned
band

_____

_____

_____

## berry
bury

_____

_____

_____

## B

### brake
break

_____

_____

_____

### break
brake

_____

_____

_____

### bury
berry

_____

_____

_____

## B

### buy
by, bye

_____

_____

_____

### by
buy, bye

_____

_____

_____

### bye
buy, by

_____

_____

_____

**Sound Alikes**

# C
## cell
sell

_____

_____

_____

_____

## cent
scent, sent

_____

_____

_____

_____

# E
## eight
ate

_____

_____

_____

_____

# F
## farther
father

_____

_____

_____

## father
farther

_____

_____

_____

## find
fined

_____

_____

_____

# F
## fined
find

_____

_____

_____

## flour
flower

_____

_____

_____

## flower
flour

_____

_____

_____

GHIJKL

# G
## guessed
guest

_____

_____

_____

## guest
guessed

_____

_____

_____

# H
## heard
herd

_____

_____

_____

## herd
heard

_____

_____

_____

## hi
high

_____

_____

_____

# H
## high
hi

_____

_____

_____

_____

# I
## its
it's

_____

_____

_____

_____

## it's
its

_____

_____

_____

_____

**GHIJKL**

# K
## knew
new

_____

_____

_____

# K
## knows
nose

_____

_____

_____

## knight
night

_____

_____

_____

## know
no

_____

_____

_____

# L
## lead
led

_____

_____

_____


## led
lead

_____

_____

_____


# M
## mail
male

_____

_____

_____


## male
mail

_____

_____

_____


## meat
meet

_____

_____

_____

MNOPQuRS

M

**meet**
meat

_____

_____

_____

_____

M

**missed**
mist

_____

_____

_____

_____

**mind**
mined

_____

_____

_____

_____

**mist**
missed

_____

_____

_____

_____

**mined**
mind

_____

_____

_____

_____

MNOPQuRS

# N

**new**
knew

_____

_____

_____

_____

**night**
knight

_____

_____

_____

_____

**no**
know

_____

_____

_____

_____

# N

**nose**
knows

_____

_____

_____

_____

MNOPQuRS

# O
## oh
owe

_____

_____

_____

_____

## owe
oh

_____

_____

_____

_____

# P
## pail
pale

_____

_____

_____

_____

## pale
pail

_____

_____

_____

_____

## peace
piece

_____

_____

_____

_____

Wilson Fundations® | ©2005, 2012 Wilson Language Training Corporation

MNOPQuRS

# P

## piece
peace

_____

_____

_____

## plain
plane

_I Just a plain_
_kid_

_____

_____

## plane
plain

_The plane is_
_about to land_

_____

# P

## principal
principle

_____

_____

_____

## principle
principal

_____

_____

_____

# R
## right
write

*you don't know if you are right or not!*

# S
## sail
sale

_____

_____

_____

_____

## sale
sail

_____

_____

_____

_____

## scene
seen

_____

_____

_____

_____

S

# scent
cent, sent

_____

_____

_____

# seen
scene

_____

_____

_____

# sell
cell

_____

_____

_____

S

# sent
cent, scent

_____

_____

_____

# side
sighed

_____

_____

_____

# sighed
side

_____

_____

_____

## S

### some
sum

_____

_____

_____

_____

### son
sun

_____

_____

_____

_____

### stationary
stationery

_____

_____

_____

_____

## S

### stationery
stationary

_____

_____

_____

_____

### straight
strait

_____

_____

_____

_____

### strait
straight

_____

_____

_____

_____

**MNOPQuRS**

# S

## sum
some

_____

_____

_____

## sun
son

_____

_____

_____

# T

## their
there, they're

_____

_____

_____

## there
their, they're

_____

_____

_____

## they're
their, there

_____

_____

_____

**TUVWXYZ**

**TUVWXYZ**

# T
## throne
thrown

_____

_____

_____

## thrown
throne

_____

_____

_____

# W
## wait
weight

_____

_____

_____

## warn
worn

_____

_____

_____

## weak
week

_____

_____

_____

W

# wear
where

_____

_____

_____

_____

# weather
whether

_____

_____

_____

_____

# week
weak

_____

_____

_____

_____

W

# weight
wait

_____

_____

_____

_____

# where
wear

_____

_____

_____

_____

# whether
weather

_____

_____

_____

_____

**TUVWXYZ**

W

## which
witch

Which one shoud I take?

W

## write
right

Don't you need to write your name?

## witch
which

✗ Help its a witch!

## worn
warn

TUVWXYZ